A LIFE WORTH LIVING

A LIFE WORTH LIVING

A Collection Of Poetry

NICHOLAS KAUFMANN

Charleston, SC
www.PalmettoPublishing.com

A Life Worth Living
Copyright © 2023 by Nicholas Kaufmann

First Edition

Hardcover ISBN: 979-8-8229-2780-3
Papberback ISBN: 979-8-8229-2781-0

TRIGGER WARNING

This book contains and describes sensitive topics such as eating disorders, mental illnesses, and suicidal thoughts and themes. If any of these themes cause extreme discomfort, I would recommend that you proceed carefully and or do not read the book thank you.

HAVEN'T WRITTEN

I haven't written in a while
Cause it all just sounds like bile
Spewing from my mouth in hopes to compile
Some poems or raps
Lyrics that rhyme and don't sound like ass

Anyway I'm getting off topic
Not explaining why I haven't dropped some bomb shit
I've had a year of complete isolation
And I'm getting tired of contemplation
About why I suck and everyone's better
Fuck I've even used the analogy of a sweater

To show that I'm a little bit down
And I've been acting like one hell of a clown
Joking and laughing about my destruction
Rhyming about it to show at the function

So I guess I'm uninspired
All the mini me's in my head got fired
And all my ideas went up in the pyre
Making my mind a mire

I haven't written in a while
Cause I've lost it
My flow got flossed out
And I'm washed up
Frankly I've just gotta stop it
Come to terms I won't drop some hot shit
And just drop it

LOOKING FOR RICHES

I'm a cadaver
As cold as ever
Left with things that really don't matter

Worthless and rusted
Eroded and encrusted
Were the only things I've been trusted

She's a grave robber
Looking for riches
Hoping for some bloke or misses

Ornate corpses engraved skulls
Things that could fix economic lulls

I'm just a cadaver
Lowly in stature
But id do anything to have her

Dig me up and take me home
Put me on a shelf bone by bone

She's gotten the rich ones
Kings lords and vassals
The rest of us aren't worth the hassle

Yet she encroaches ever closer
To my flimsy wooden enclosure

Getting closer every night
Hoping her pickaxe might
Hit something worth the stakes

But the more I watch the less she takes
I mean king Phillip really only ate steaks
Yet she left him and his mates

And came over to me
Dug me up
And set me free

Flickering lights hit my corpse
And I think she'll skip over me of course

Yet she stays marveling and inspecting
Like she's fully expecting
This to be the end of her woes
To not just have to roll with the blows

And lights up instantly
Almost insistently

Leaving all her treasure around
As she rips me violently from the ground

She's caught and taken away
All my hopes gone in a day
That's the 7th one this may

As I'm sure she is being misused
And I'm sure she'll end up like me soon

Just another corpse in the gutter
Waiting for a grave robber to tear them asunder

From this rot land and ground
Oh look there's another one now

He's a grave robber
Looking for riches
Hoping for some bloke or misses

RAIN

I love the rain
The sound it makes the smell
And the way it looks on my window panes
It reminds me of a time when I had growing pains

When I was younger
Smaller and humbler
When I didn't have a coffee filled tumbler

So I could get up at four
To get that pump before
A day filled with work and agitation
Filled with temptation

To cut out and quit
To just say that's it
And be done
To be shunned

By myself and others
What Id give to go back just a couple of summers

When I didn't care
About my flair or weight
Wait guys I'm falling behind
I feel like I'm out of my mind

Left inside for years
To let all my fears
Manifest and erode
Leaving it to all explode
Ruining my life
God what Id do to be done with this strife

To just see the rain
And let it all pour
To not feel insane
And not worry anymore

God I miss the rain
The sounds it makes the smell
The lack of shame
When you tripped and fell

LAST MAN ON EARTH

The last man on Earth
Hears a knock on his door
And he wonders what all the noise is for

It's far too late to go outside
And far too early to say he tried
So he might as well just stay inside

Forget all the knocking
The clutter the noise
Stay locked away with a semblance of poise

Ignore all attempts
For salvation and help
It wouldn't matter since he didn't do it himself

To suffer is joy
And pain is admired
The last man on earth was truly inspired

By the knocking on his door
And the thought occurred to him
I could do this once more

Help is for the weak
And perseverance the stronger
And he thought I could do this much longer

Sit in here all day
With the rest of the world at bay
Rolling with what may

Come of this dismal life
Strengthened by eternal strife
Of the last man on Earth

The last man on Earth
Was a very lonely man
Before the days were gone
And the population turned to sand
He never could seem to land

He was stubborn and quite uptight
And things never seemed to go quiet right
But a man of standards he was
Never fell or needed help because
He was brought up right

The last man on Earth
Was a strong believer in that
Belief never faltered or cracked
And he knew that
he must be rewarded
But as days went on it just got morbid

So the last man on Earth
Heard a knock on his door
And he decided he just couldn't take it any more

Got up from his seat
Built off lies and deceit
And went up to the door
Discarding what he learned before

What was hammered in from years of education
Gone without a second thought or hesitation
And opened the door

Hoping to find what he's always been looking for
More then a quiet exception
Born form internal acception

That he must suffer
For whatever reason
And to have a buffer
Would be close to treason

He was so excited to see
What the door would hold for him
Opened it with glee
Hoping to would be a new mold of him

But the last man on Earth
Heard the knocking no more
A deafening silence only for

The stubborn man who was trapped in his ways
An empty door frame with a maniacal gaze
Left the last man on earth in a dizzying daze

As he remembered
To suffer is coy
And pain is a mire
The last man on earth was only a liar

To himself and others
And he realizes now
The knocking on the door
Was his only way out

And he ignored it for years
Convinced he was alone
The last man on earth
Was never on his own

LOVE

I've never had the time to do what I wanted
Found my passion and love unrequited
Found my progress and achievement slighted
Which really might've

Took me down
Killed me without a sound
With no other way around
But a coffin six feet in the ground

Or sent me away to a compound
Just without the joy of a fracture
With a little tight coat and come down
That might've really helped with my stature

Or posture
And I'm starting to feel a little like an imposter
Because I foster
Ideas I can't fathom
With an unbelievable belief I can grab em

But I've never had the time to be what I wanted
A famous idol that's only a little haunted
Or a Grecian God with abs I could've flaunted
But given the time allotted

I really didn't do that bad
I mean I could've gone insane or mad
Never found love and be glad
That I'm clad

In my makeup and clothes
Wake up and face the day
With only minimal woes
Be able to look at myself and say
Your not the worst person you know
And it's really starting to show

So I guess I've had the time I needed
To be a version of me that really succeeded
To be a little less petty and conceited
And to finally feel I deserve a seat in
Every room I've been seen in

ICARUS

Used to be like Icarus
So happy I could fly
But whenever I think of us
I get more and more shy

Used to have wings
Be free as a bird
But now nothing about me sings
Nothing saying a word

Used to be like Icarus
Didn't care what people said
But now whenever I think of us
I feel like I would do better dead

Whenever I think of us
I feel like we've got worse
Me myself and I
Could really use some work

It's happening again
A shift in my writing
It all sounds the same
With the occasional sighting

Of something new
And worthwhile
But mainly skewed
To a pile of bile

I never could write
Not even a few lines
At this point I might
Just stop to save the time

Do something productive
Leave it to the professionals
Because it's more destructive
Then a cup of methanol

Another poem about pain
One about being a dick
It's truly a shame
I haven't just quit

But I'm too stubborn to stop
Because I need it
To uptight about my slop
I guess I'm conceited

Since I haven't conceded
Or abdicated my throne
I share at every meeting
Because I need it to be shown

To someone who isn't me
Someone who might like my writing
Because I still can't see
The problems that I'm fighting

Whether it be my appearance
The mold of imperfection
Or like it's on clearance
An ode to my reflection

But I appreciate the meetings
The hearts on the line
I'm a big fan of feelings
As long as it's timed

But I really do love poetry
I just hate the way I write
I guess woe is me
If I can't get the bar just right

If it's half baked
Or just bullshit
I guess for my sake
I just have to push it

So it's happening again
Like a shift in lighting
The sparks not the same
But I guess I'll keep writing

POSSIBILITIES

I wanna be a player but I'd get too attached
I wanna hand on the world and a hand on her ass
Then I realize as she starts to runs on past
I can't stop thinking about the vast

Possibilities I could have with this girl
I could spend all my time with her and show her the world
At this point I might as well just give it a whirl

But you see it's a process
A promise to give her everything in the world and not less
And I've realized I'm a lot less heartless

Then I would need to be to be a player
Because I've never thought to play her
And really it's just a lot of layers
Of confusion

An illusion of grandeur
That I'd be able to hand her
All that she wanted on a silver plate
Take my hand off the world and keep it on her beautiful
frame

Never let go or ever be the same
And I know that it's such a shame
That I get so attached
And I've hatched

Every scheme to get better
But every time I just can't let her

Go to live her life
Free from me
Free from strife
And I still don't know what she could see

In a possible player like me

I haven't ran in awhile
Not even just a short mile
I'm just stuck inside a pile
Of nothing
Combusting
At the seems to do something

I haven't won in a while either
And the clock is ticking like a Geiger
And if this goes on I might find myself on the bottom of
an alcoholic cider

Rotting away day by day
Strangled by an overwhelming sense of dismay

What am I doing
Pursuing
Something I don't love
That doesn't fit like a glove
Working just to get payed
And I'm starting to feel insane
Looking at the same four walls
With the same voices echoing in these halls

Of my mind
Asking what am I going to find
In this career or major
I really just want to end up like Bill Hader

But that's not gonna happen
And that's the problem I'm trapped in
I really wanna get into acting
But my payment is gonna be lacking

I can't pursue my passion
Because I don't wanna eat out a trashcan
And that's my problem that's my problem

I'm too much of a dreamer to give it up
But I got the ego of a streamer to not give a fuck

About the money
And it's funny
If I believed in myself I would go for it
Jump off that edge and make a show of it
But I don't

I got the flair of a dramatic
And the ability to spit bars and lines that would kill an
asthmatic

But I just don't believe in myself
And no one else does
And when I ask about it I just get fuzz
Or fuss and I've already gotten so much

That I don't think I could do it
Change my career and be like shit I blew it

Four years down the drain
And I'm less then a grain
Of sand to anyone that matters
And I'd be flattered to get a job as a teacher or waiter
Be a kiss ass with every sentence ending with okay sir

So I gotta stick with something that I hate
A malignant growth I can't amputate
Which is really just aper poe
Because I just wanna go
From anything medical
Which is really starting to sound heretical

To anyone I talk to
And I'm locked to
This sinking ship
And no one seems to give a shit

But it's fine
It's cool I'll make it work
Shut up and stop being such a twerp
About it
Because I use every chance to shout it
To everyone around
Till they're practically buried underground

And maybe that's why it's frowned upon
Why all my complaints are a drop of water in a pond
Because I've pawned away
Every dismay
To anyone that's willing to say hey

But like I said it's fine
I'll deal with it
Hell I'll find a way to heal with it
Spend some time with my major
And then write a line like I'm stuck in a manger

Be one stupid bloke with a job
That he hates but at least it'll get the mob
On it's reigns while I get a lobotomy
Because I know in the heart of me
It's not what I want to do but boo hoo
For you is the response I'll get

So for awhile
I'll sit here
With this fear
That I'm going to hate my career
And do nothing about it

Because I haven't cared in a while
About my passions or love
But instead the pile
Is all I'm thinking of

SOMEONE LIKE ME

What's a little cut
To someone like me
Pushed down in the gutter till he couldn't see
Was told he was fat since he was three
And maybe that's what made me me

So what's a little slight
to someone like me
Someone who might
Exclaim they were free
Till about every night
Where he wishes he could be
Just a bit more light on his feet

So what's a little fight
To someone like me
Would starve every night
So that he could be
Closer to someone like me

Gaunt and skinny
Was what we needed
Such a pity
That we conceded

Just so we might
Feel a little less tired
Gave up your plight
We could've been admired

You were doing so great
Barely eating a meal
Barely feeling irate
Let alone feel

Nothing could get to you
You were strong as steel
Think of what it meant to you
Till you let them steal
All of it away
One fateful day
When you decided to say
Hey

I'm a hundred pounds and five eleven
And barely eat around seven
calories a day
If we include what I throw away

You could never be
someone like me
An ideal picture
For all to see

You're weak
And you know it
You had what you seek
And you had to throw it

Down the drain
With your brain
And all those thoughts
That made you better
Now you'll never
Be what you've always wanted
See what you could've flaunted

Now you're careless
You eat like a pig
You'll be peerless
When you get so big

And you know it
And I do too
So much so that you want to tow it
Up from the place you threw it

Polish it up and make it new
Be so much more than bland old you

Fine I won't get you today
But I know one day you'll crack
And come crawling back
Wishing you could be
Even close to someone like me

PERFECTION A TRUE VILLANELLE

Perfection
More to do
Less to mention

Obsession
I would say you
Actual Perfection

Pure tension
When we say adieu
More to mention less to do

Accession
Of my heart rates true
Because perfection is only you

No more to mention
Even less to do
Perfection
Is less to mention to you

FUCKED UP

I think I fucked up
And I'm really scared
Don't know if I can makeup
Might have bared
A bit too much

Frayed the last nerve
Lit the last fuse
Forced her to serve
Just hope she doesn't choose
To break it off

I couldn't really blame her
Not even a scoff or sigh
Never would shame her
It wouldn't even matter why
If she were to leave

I don't know how I'd make it
I'd really have to try
Surely would have to fake it
To barely even cry
Always thought I would say goodbye

And maybe that's the problem
Was too much of a narcissist
Didn't realize I could harm them
If I made all my problems first

Made our time together
About me
Made us farther
And I didn't see
How much of a prick I was

So I think I fucked up
With minimal chance of repair
Was much less of a hiccup
And more gasping for air

SWEET DISSOLUTION

The service your providing
Is like a five course dinner
With the poison and knifes your hiding
Flourished with an awful demeanor

And I love it but you don't see her
With a love I covet that hurts like a cleaver
And despite all that I still can't leave her

Trapped in a game
Like a pawn to a king
Filled with pain
That's suited for her liking

Each play a step
Curated for her amusement
Ever closer to check
What I'd give for such awful dissolution

I miss it the pain she provided
How I longed to run away
With every attempt slighted
Keeping my sanity at bay

Rambling and bickering
You might call it fighting
The light of my life flickering
I call it exciting

Complements and flattery
Were demeaning at best
Assault and battery
Oh please say yes

I'm at home in a game
Like a king to a queen
It would truly be a shame
If I ever were to wean

Myself back from the edge
Of my insanity
Break my own pledge
To the only thing that's mattered to me

Eternal service
For as long as we're living
You might get nervous
But I just do her bidding

I just have a feeling
That I won't outlive her
I find it quite befitting
That I'm more like chopped liver

I won't be here much longer
Especially when duty calls
I saw her with a prong or
Maybe something with claws

So this is probably good bye
Awful absolution
And I'll finally ride that high
Of sweet dissolution

HELL HATH NO FURY

Abused by a kiss
Comforted by shame
Amused by a shift
Of loving to pain

It always turns sour
But that's what I prefer
As I count every long hour
For her to differ

To the spiteful way she speaks to me
The venom on her tongue
And then it's clear to see
She must be the one

For me to be with
To spend all my time
To be under a guillotine
Would be beautifully divine

Have my head on a platter
Go with the blows
Nothing else would matter
As long as it's only mine that rolls

I crave her attention
It's the only thing I want
Just a little mention
And everything else could rot

Hell hath no fury
Like a woman scorned
There's no hurry
I've already been warned

I'm ready for the abuse
And I'll take it on the chin
With steady misuse
We can both call it a win

And no it's no capital of Sweden
Cause I'm not the hostage
It's more like a battle I've been in
With frankly to little losses

I'm abused by a shift
From pain to love
Frankly adrift
Because it's not what I'm thinking of

I don't want the kisses
And adoration
I just want the misses
And amputation

I don't want it to work
Or get better
I just want to serve
And frankly just let her

Use me for what I'm worth
And show it to the world
Leave me with a dearth
Of anything but curled

Fists and sharp knives
Cause that's what excites
The loss of my life
And flickering lights

And frankly you're a bore
When you're not at my neck
I just need so much more
Then someone who'll check

On how I'm doing
And what I want
I just want someone who's pursuing
Me for every taunt

So I guess I'll wait
For this to turn sour
For the venom to be replaced
and me devoured

Because hell hath no fury
Like a woman scorned
And there's no jury
For this to be adjourned

So Ill wait to be abused by a hit
And comforted by pain
Because the fires already been lit
In every corner of my brain

And I can't let go
And neither can you
I just want you to show
What you really want to do

Tie me up
And make me plead no more
Maybe a cut
Paired with a fine Pinot noir

I won't tell you what to do
But it can't be this
I just have such an issue
With you greeting me with a kiss

Just something please
To remind me of the past
That will indefinitely leave
Me suffering in a cast

Or I might have to leave
Cut it off with you
Unless you cleave
Me right in two

A knife to the back
Or the carotid artery
That'll cause a snap
Right in the heart of me

Rekindle my love
Like you did long ago
Be the only one I'm thinking of
Remind me of the blows

No
Are you sure
Oh
Well Ill show myself to the door

I did love you
But just with the knives
I guess I lost sight of you
When I didn't lose my life

HOPE

I've lost it
I just don't feel the same
Accosted
Between insanity and sane

A mountain
Of insufferable pain
A fountain
Of useless refrains

And rebuttals
Which is just there to muddle
The situation at hand
Which I struggle to talk about like any other man

I've lost it
And I don't know how to pay
The debts that are surely on the way
Because I've borrowed to much to even say

I've lost it
Any semblance of poise
Anything I put out is just useless noise
And I don't know where I'm going
And I'm scared
Frankly impaired by the lack of a choice

For once in my life I'm put on a one way track
Only looking forward no way back
With no plan or tact
And only flak
For me alone to deal with

I don't know what to say
No poetic ending
No triumphant hurray
Devoid of anything
worthy of a soiree

I've lost it
The part of me that dreamed
I've tossed it
In the nearest dirty latrine

Because it didn't do anything now
What will it do in the future
I've truly learned how
To be one apathetic loser

Who can't even put on an illusion
Of weak and frail smile
Who's artistic delusions
Just always turn to bile

UNFORTUNATE
THOUGHTS

I've had some unfortunate thoughts
Not intrusive
Or exclusive
But more inclusive

Of my demise
My death so to speak
Which seems to signal I've reached a peak
In my unfortunate mental streak

Of strain it seems I can handle
Since I see every ledge as a mantle
And every sharp object a sample
Of life that could never be

A life ending catastrophe
But as I was saying it has to be
Some obstacle in my way
Something left to weigh

On my soul
Like a part of me that just isn't whole
That is devoid like a shole or crater

And if I could have one little favor
It would be to have something cater
To this unfortunate though theatre
Or theater

Either would be suitable
Since everyday day it plays this inscrutable
Demented series of events
With little or no pretense
And it's intense
To see myself die
With little explaining itself why

Either I'm painting the wall like a Picasso painting
Or I'm jumping of the roof contemplating

My mortality
And what it means to me in totality
I just don't see the reality in this situation
The reason for finality in this altercation

I don't see myself doing it
I mean I do in the moment
A fleeting flash of something despondent
A couple of seconds where my mind went
To some dark and dismal place
Where I'm not well met

And at this point I'm hell bent
On finding the reason
And I feel asking for help would be treason
And I don't know why I refuse to fix this irritating little
lesion

I'm scared
That I know what it is
And I don't want them to hear
That I've caved to every fear
Gave in to it all
I just can't make that jump
Or fall

So I've had some unfortunate thoughts
And I really can't face them
I've tried every scheme
Made up too many plots
I've tried to find the hem
Stich up every seem
And I'm lost
To so many unfortunate thoughts

I WANNA

I wanna get hit by an expensive car
Get a good injury
Something above par
So I could stand in front of a jury

And exclaim my pain
And reap all the rewards
To place all the blame
And get the awards

I wanna distance myself
From all my choices and acts
To not listen to myself
And be much more lax

Like an unreliable narrator
Of a second person story
Be a broken down elevator
Never restored to it's former glory

Can't move up or elevate
But I can't descend
Which is nice to extenuate
The inevitable end

I wanna live in an admirable stagnence
Or stagnation
To strive in an endless absence
Forever in jubilation

To strive in consistency
And condemn change
Move forward aimlessly
Never turning a page

I don't want a life
That is filled with strife
And the more then occasional strain

Don't want to deal with the drain
That cuts through like a knife
Or the repetitive mundane

I wanna live in one moment
Forever
To be able to hold it
Whatever

It is that I feel I need
And stay there happy
Not needing to plead
Or feel so crappy

I wanna live in a line
That I mold to perfection
That occupies my mind
Forever viewing the reflection

Of something worthwhile
Something I crave
Something worthy of a smile
And maybe even praise

I need to write
I don't wanna write
I need too it's simple

Otherwise it's irritated
And rises like a pimple
Makes me infuriated
And then I cant keep cool

And ruins me
And yes
Do I have a litany
Of press

Or papers
That express
My endless capers

And expeditions into my depth
Of emotions
That still impress
Me on how far I can push the notion

Of sadness
Or woe
Of madness
To show

That I'm stuck in a cycle
Of my own creation
The stagnence I idol
Is my limitation

And that's it
My fatal flaw
We've hit
My hamartia

My one endless sorrow
That I keep repeating
The tragedy of tomorrow
That keeps me reading

The same tired lines
And worn out themes
The over used rhymes
That only seems

To say the same thing
In a different order
Each time with less meaning
And I'm on the border

The end of my writing
How much farther I can go
Constantly fighting
My want to let go

To just stop writing in general
To fade away
Like I was ephemeral

And I don't know how to end this
I never really do
I just keep writing till there's something new

And maybe that's the problem

HONORABLE PARIAH

I miss the emptiness
The loss of joy
The endless weariness
Strung along like a toy

The inability to move on
The remnants of my past
The joy of holding on
Remembering how the die were cast

A painful nostalgia
A joyous little cut
The honorable pariah
Of a comforting rut

Where I'm stuck
And can't get out
Enjoying the muck
Of this endless drought

ARTISTRY

And it's crazy
How everything is turning hazy
It's just not the way
See I thought I'd be something better
Write lyrics and rhymes that were weter
But weather isn't always damp
And whether I keep writing I'll always be drawn to the
lamp
The light at the end of the tunnel
Where I'll inevitably fumble
And find myself at the business end of a pummel

What I'm saying is I can't succeed
But I can't secede
Because I've already planted a seed in my mind
Saying there's something to find in this mess
And whether it's for stress
Or a way to decompress
I have to keep going and say it from the chest

The problem is my best won't always be great
In fact most of the time its barely half rate
And every bad line makes me irritate
And I've yet to write a rhyme that puts me in that state

Of euphoria and bliss
Where the lines never miss
And I'm happy with the way that I write
And I'm put on a path that has a sight
Of a future that's bright and cheerful
Instead of the one I'm on where I'm lonely and fearful

That this is all that I have
A desperate attempt to be more then half
Of what I want to be
A last ditch attempt to hold on to the artistry
That I feel has made me, me
But I'm stuck and in the heart of me

I know that it is what I've said
Something I cling to so I don't end up dead
Something that should be more then what's in my head
But it's not

And I don't think it will be
At least at the moment I can't see it clearly
Hell I'm writing this drunk
Because apparently all of this emotion sunk
To some depth of my soul and just shrunk

Into a ball of destruction and fear
Where I'm teetering on the pier
Of the unknown
The oblivion
Where the only thing I see is stygian
And eldritch in nature

And maybe I can't comprehend
The problems I seem to send
Myself into full steam ahead
And if I had half a brain
Or a good head on my shoulders
I'd see that these problems are like Sisyphean boulders

An impossible challenge
I go through daily
And the best face I put on is sick
And palely

And it's a wonder I haven't gone crazy
But at this point I may see
The closest thing to psychiatry
I'll get a padded vest
Where I can invest
My time into something productive
A shift in paradigm to be more inductive

Of something more illustrious
To focus on something more industrious
To make a living and be known as the best of us

And it's crazy
How I used to be so lazy
And let every little thing phase me
I used to be so in tune with my emotion
And now I have to dive into this ocean
Of lies and deceit
To even get one hundred feet
To how I really feel

And even then it all feels like trill
Something I want to hear that will let me fill
Another page in my notes
Of barely passable poetry
But at this point that's how I know it's me
Every last ditch attempt to put out a bit of artistry

To try to explain what I am to me
To try and find what I aim to be
In the endless monotony
In my desperate hunt for artistry

AND MAYBE

And maybe that's all it was meant to be
A desperate attempt to stave off lunacy
Since I don't see any adoration or balloons for me

And maybe it could've been a future
One with bright lights that would suture
This worrying fear that I'm just a loser

And maybe it wasn't meant to be
Anything more than an attempt to see
A different happier side of me

And maybe I should've known that from the start
Enjoyed it for what it was instead of breaking my heart
Searching endlessly for a part

And maybe I would've been happier
If I wasn't stuck in the moments after first
And I didn't pass or lurch

On every opportunity handed to me
And maybe I was blind to see
The joy of artistry

And maybe I never understood
The meaning of being stood
On stage in front of the masses
Performing through glasses
Or frames doing it for the joy not the fame

And maybe that's why it never happened
Because I stopped and dampened
My entire dream to a paycheck
Stopped the scene for a raincheck

All that mattered was the salary
The numbers and zeros became my reality
And encompassed my life in totality

And maybe that why it turned out the way it did
Stuck in an endless loop wishing to be a kid
But I can't kid myself any longer
Because right now I'm just a monger
Whining all day as I ponder
The what ifs and maybes a little bit longer

AS OF YESTERDAY

I'm single as of yesterday
And that's just how it goes
Don't have to much to say
I just go where the wind blows

I guess it's an art
That as of yesterdays heart
Didn't ever learn till the start
Of something new

And I knew that as of yesterday
She'd be gone
Some say It'd be less to pay
But they'd be wrong

I guess it's a mark
That as of yesterday harks
A new beginning and remarks
There's just no more sparks

And as of yesterday
Even though she's gone
I figured there'd be hell to pay
But I'm only moving on

Only looking forward
To the yesterdays of tomorrow
Moving ever stalwart
With no time to borrow

And as of yesterday I was less
And so was she
Though we both loved each other's caress
We both had to leave

And as of yesterday I was weak
Clinging on so desperately
But now I'm not so meek
Without my own mind to mess with me

And as of yesterday she wasn't happy
Never wanting better
But now she's been set free
Because she finally let her

And yesterday is gone
And tomorrow is all that matters
So I'll repeat this song
When all else falls to tatters

BLURRY

I feel aimless
And blurry
Like I'm not going anywhere in a hurry

I feel shameless
And worry
That this is the end of me surely

I need to talk to someone
But it can't be you
I wish it could be but that time is overdue

And I'm exhausted
But I can't fall asleep
And I think I've lost it
I didn't think I'd take the fall so steep

I can't keep coming back
And it's nothing you do
It's just the odds are so stacked
To always favor you

And I'd savor
Every moment we had
And like a paver
We could block out the bad

But that's all far gone
And we both know that
But I can't seem to hold back
For all that long

I'm doing much better
I'm cooking and eating
But like a fletcher
Every thing I make is sent careening

To be shot forward
Ephemeral and fleeting
To be lost and lowered
From any real meaning

I have such highs and lows without you
Which is something I haven't really felt
But I can tell you just because it's new
Doesn't mean it doesn't hurt or pelt

Me with distractions
And emptiness

It's the heartbreak that hurts
And it's the hope that kills
That we could find a hint of normalcy
Tucked far away in the hills

It's the fact that you've moved on
And want a normal friendship
But I'm still the pawn
To our sudden split

And it's me
And I know that
I feel so blurry
And I still lack

The control I want
And I don't know what to do
I can't loose the muscle memory
As fast as I lost you

NYQUIL

NyQuil vodka and melatonin
And I've gone melancholic
It won't be much longer till I phone in
But don't worry the NyQuil's nonalcoholic

So it's fine
Is what I'm saying
There's no visible decline
Or unhealthy habit I'm displaying

I just wanted to call
To see how you were doing
To see if your still in the fall
Or if your pursuing

Something new
Mainly someone
Hey hey this is about you
Just wanted to know if you've had fun

No particular reason
Just need, wanted to know
Why? Your acting like this is treason
I just wanted to show

Something I'm not sure
How am I doing
What did you need a brochure
I'm obviously moving

On or forward how ever

You want to put it
I'm obviously not never
Gonna get through it

Any plans
To occupy your time
No demands
Or needs on your mind

Why do you keep turning this back to me
I'm the one asking the questions
Cause it's obvious to see
That there's some tensions

Oh no
Puft why would there be tension
That's a low blow
Considering my intentions

Wanting to call you up
With everything on my plate
Look I'm sorry if this interrupts
Whatever you're doing making you irate

Why won't I let up
Because I'm livid
I feel like I've been set up
When the whole thing was so vivid

Sorry I guess I'm a little hung up
On the whole thing
And I haven't oh she hung up
That's one hell of a sting

DOWN TO EARTH

Lets just see where this goes
As you go on I work on my prose
I mean my verse not my cons or pros
I just want a down to Earth kinda verse

I just want a down to earth kinda verse
A sad and melancholic beat where I'm adverse
To any help that you provide and it's a feat
How far I'll sink, inches miles feet

It don't matter as long as I leak
Any semblance of me
On the hot pavement street
A neat little puddle
Of muddled mumbled verses
As the onlookers call the hearses
Cause the social services

Couldn't stop the sink
And God knows I could use a shrink
To let all the shitty things that I think out

In a meaningful way
Instead a shitty verse where I don't pay
Attention to the words making things worse

Cause I spit it to my friends while thinking I'm down to Earth
Even though we're in the same room they look like they are
in Perth

And I can't tell you what any of this is worth
Forcefully looking away to make it worse
So I can write some prose a verse
I don't know where it goes and it hurts

To turn away from anyone that cares
Dropping out of the mind of peers in pairs
Cause I can't make up my mind I'm here and there
And I still don't want to hear what's fair

And as I go on I work on my flow
Compiling rhymes and things I should know
But as I search I find I don't have more
Things to write about other then my poor

Mental health and frankly impeccable flow state
Lack of wealth and my senseless ability to inflate
Any menial problem to a life and death scenario
I want to be down to Earth but it's scary so
I exaggerate
And stay in a hell I make
So I can flake
On any activity that might accentuate the positive

But I'm in the negatives
For my mood and the hells I give
To try and get better

I want a down to Earth kinda verse
To target the cancers the problems that make me worse
But I don't know what it's worth

PITCH

I find myself hiding from the truth
Loving the lie
As I relax in a booth
Parched and mouth dry

Waiting in a suit and tie
To sell you my pitch
Explaining why
Sleeping together won't be a bitch

Where we wake up in the morning
Refreshed and pristine
Never grieving or mourning
And cut if off clean

Exclaiming I'm safe dick
We won't get attached
Plus you wouldn't mind a quick lick
It's not like we'll get latched

Together in this endeavor
That we pursue
Despite our best effort
To find someone new

I wait patiently
As you mull it over
And smile complacently
As you say fuck it come over

I find myself hiding from the truth
As I lie in your bed
Figured I'd be a little more loose
But I spiral in my head

You said I love you
And I said it back
I should've said fuck you
As I ran out the back

But I lack
Any real defenses
The odds are stacked
And you swing for the fences

And hit it out the park
Every time
Igniting a spark
In my mind

Cause a combustion
That I've never seen
Lead to Influx
Of the same damn dream

Which is more of a nightmare
But that being said
You never did fight fair

But I can't be mad
I set this up
I can't be sad
I texted you up

But I love the lie
Saying I'm fine
Never elaborate why
Just biding my time

Till the morning
Where you call me baby
Without any warning
And lately
Even though I'm scoring
I think it's more like I'm mourning

I find myself hiding from the truth
As I text you a place and a when
Not knowing what I have to lose
Or maybe not caring again

Cause I love the lie
As I lie on your sheets
I'll vie for attention
Till the night just repeats

The I love you
The same
The I miss you
And pain
The pet names
And shame

I find myself hiding from the truth
Because I love the lie
As I sit there prepared in a booth
For the pitch of a lonely guy

THORNS

I'll pick the thorns
So you can hold the roses with no fears
Flowers to adorn
Our love and relationship to peers

I'll take the wounds
The cuts and scares
Wont heal real soon
But it's worth the tears

A beautiful crimson
Of blood and flower
A pitiful hymn sung
Of love to tower

It'll be a symbol
Of strength and prosperity
It'll be a hymnal
At length of dexterity

How far I'll go
To fix a crumbling foundation
How long I'll tow
With a bubbling fixation

Of pure perfection
Not caving to vexation
A broken reflection
Not focusing on causation

I'll feel the pain
So you can be happy
All in vain
For you to out lap me

I'll take the prick
And be one to boot
Cut to the quick
All points being moot

I'll say I tried
And you say I know
A part of me died
When we said hello

Long after we split
We were just too inviting
We should've just quit
And stopped confiding

I'll be the one to take it
Each question each blow
And just try to fake it
So subtle vexation doesn't show

I'll be the thorn
To be the one you hate
Filled with anger and scorn
Just to accentuate

The reason you should leave
And find someone better
I can't let her grieve
I won't be a tether

I wish I was the rose
The beautiful flower
Only what shows
Is all that would matter

But I'll be the thorn
So you can be free
Giving you no time to mourn
The loss of me

ANSWER

I'll use my final days for an answer
A question of the malaise
To try and find the root of this cancer
That metastasized in days

That started in my cardiac tract
And moved up to the brain
Wishing that I could have just seconds back
But it wouldn't stop the pain

I'll use my final days for enjoyment
As much as I can at least
Before I get the adornment
When my breathings finally ceased

Try and find the joy
In the days of paying
Play around and toy
With the motion of a candle swaying

A flicker at best
With the light dying steadily
All my wrongs confessed
To try and be heavenly

I'll use my final days to realize
I don't want an answer
Put in perspective and conceptualize
My life as a meaningless dancer

Never caring about my problems
Or wanting the solution
Never attempting to solve them
Just craving dissolution

SINCE WE SPLIT

I don't have much to say
I want to get back together
When there wasn't hell to pay
And the days were much better

Instead of what I have
This endless oblivion
The only thing in my nav
Making me think again

About the past
Before we split
Before even CAST
When I was ready to quit

I moved and it was hard
I had nothing going
I moved still scarred
But I saw you glowing

In the corner of a class
That I wasn't even gonna take
I just wanted an easy pass
But by far my best mistake

Because I met you
In such unlikely circumstances
But for once I knew
I had no chances

We'd talk and we'd flirt
Just to have some fun
But eventually quite curt
You basically asked if I was dumb

You asked if I liked you
Or if it was just a game
I found you quite cute
But dumbfounded I racked my brain

I thought about it for a day or two
Not knowing what to say
Not knowing if I could care for you
Cause I struggled to get through my day

But luckily I said the right thing
And told you of course
We had more then a fling
Our love was much more then par for the course

It took a second to get used to
Those nights in your car
With your shity Bluetooth
And our feelings not so far

I love the rain
Because of those nights
Hitting the window panes
While we sat under lights

Of stars and dim lamps
Illuminating the sky
The two of us cramped
While I decided to try

And make a move
A show of affection
I destroyed my back on the console
To get your attention

And from then on I knew it
I loved and that's what matters
But I blew it
That summer ripped it to tatters

I'm truly the one to blame
I was the start
The dimming of a flame
That burned in our hearts

And since we split
I don't have much to say
Stuck in a pit
Since the start of May

I've been okay
Could be better could be worse
But almost everyday
I'm seemingly cursed

By the way I acted
And the things I said
All of it counteracting
Me getting rest in bed

So since we've split
I've wanted to get back together
Never really wanting to quit
Even though I put up no effort

THE PRICE

I'm just smoking in the rain
Yeah I got a pen
It's not too big of a pain
I only hit it every now and again

Just once or twice
When I think of you
I guess that's just the price
For being the fool

Continual drug usage
To try and find the high
Before you said duces
And I'm just some guy

Drifting on his own
Left high and dry
Recklessly alone
Every thought ending in why

I guess it's not easy for you
I'm acting like a Martyr
You're just as blue
And probably harbor

The same feelings
Of loneliness
Left you reeling
And cleaning the mess

But I guess that's the price
Of being the fools
Left to scurry like mice
And be used like tools

But I'd pay it again
In a heartbeat or less
Give you everything and lend
My fair share of stress

TONGUE TIED

You take the sunshine
And bring in the rain
I'm perfectly tongue tied
When you cross my brain

The world moves in slow mo
When you're in the room
And I'd pay just to know
How to make you swoon

You make Shangri la
Look rather blasé
I could have it all
And still don't know what to say

Because you're an anomaly
That I can't understand
I'd give you all of me
Just for your hand

And I know this is the same
Schlock that I spread
But this time I'm sane
And this has to be said

You're not the only thing
I think about
But when you spring
In my head I just wanna shout

But it'll come out mumbled
And sound insincere
Because of how much I crumble
When I try to be clear

I feel like a record
Broken on repeat
Shackled and sheltered
Forced to keep

Replaying a song
Same cord and tune
That's gone on too long
But still feels too soon

So I go on and on
Till I scratch and repeat
The marathon
That always ends at you're feet

A COUPLE MORE MONTHS

A couple more months
Till we try again
A couple more months
Till we wish it wasn't then

A couple more months
Till I'll see you again
A couple more months
With you in my head

A couple more months
Till I might be happy
A couple more months
Clinging on so madly

A couple more months
Till it's no again
A couple more months
That I should've known again

That in a couple more months
Nothing would change
And in a couple more months
I'd be deranged

PACE

Everyone says I need to move
A change of pace
Turn and loose
All that fallen grace

End the chapter
Read a new book
Happily ever after
And all it took

Was a lie
And a campaign
A sigh
And champaign

To try and move on
Get a new view
Stop the seance
And all the voodoo

To revive a dead soul
Reignite a spark
Not accounting the toll
It'd take on the heart

Probably would benefit
My happiness and joy
But I just don't really fit
In that whole category

Since I love the dark arts
The sadness and woe
Despite my smarts
I just can't let go

So I'll go on practicing
My spells and incantations
Always lacking
Congrats and innovations

OLD

I've recently looked back at my old poems
Before I was good at writing
And I didn't have the smallest bit of timing
When writing a line that barely rhymes was exciting

It's funny cause I was extremely jaded
Poems were all sad
And wrote like happiness was overrated
And that's not bad

It's just lacking view point
Real structure
Real meaning that helps the poem not sound flustered

It's odd that I wrote so much
Cause looking back I really don't like it
And sure there were some lines that might hit
But I don't know if I would be able to cite it

Word for word like I can other poems
And I know I treat them like they're tomes
Of some religious scripture
And follow them to create some picture

Of grandeur
Or something of the sort
I need them to have some allure
Or some clever retort

For something going on in my life
So I can share every little bit of strife
In a way that I find acceptable
Like a receptacle

For all my little problems
Nicely wrapped up
Claiming that I've solved em

And it's funny again
Looking back at my old poems
Because its the same thing I write now

Boiled down it's the same structure
I'm feeling down
Or like I've lost my luster
And I can't muster

The strength to work on it
So I sit and complain
About the strife or mundane
And then end it like I'm going insane

Its just funny
Realizing there just was no change
I just took time to make sure every phrase
Was what I thought worthy of praise

FROG

The frog is a simple being
Never lying or deceiving
But instead always on some path or meaning

The frog lives in a pond
Where it sits there upon
A leaf a rock or a mound
Where it is then on bound

The frog doesn't wish for more
Then what arrives at his watery door
Making the frog never wanting or poor

The frog is never faced with disaster
At least not one he couldn't deal with then after
And think about with foolish froggish laughter

The frog never had any peers
Non among him where near his tier
As the frog had delt with his fears

At least that's what was thought
But the frog was always fraught

With worry and fear
That maybe he didn't deserve his pier

His rock and his home
That he built on his own

And maybe the frog did want more
But just wasn't committed or sure

The frog isn't as simple
As perceived
For he belittles
And sees

Himself as a toad
Masquerading in his humble abode

As some paragon of virtue
Someone loving who could never hurt you

The frog takes a while to process his thoughts
Looks in the pond recounting the spots

Of his triumphs
And losses
His lumps
And then tosses

The notion of him being a toad
For he knows he's a frog a la mode

For he was faced with disasters
That he dealt with then after

And moments of despair
Combated with laughter

And the frog realized
That it was a lack of peers in his eyes
But the rest of the wildlife idealized

The frog for being a humble being
Never hurting lying or deceiving

But instead adapting when careening
Who takes the time to give everyone meaning

From the little tadpoles in the pool
To the lizards keeping cool

The frog is a happy being
Accepting faults and a little careening
For it is the bumps and mistakes that give life meaning

THE SUN AND THE MOON

The sun rose and shone each morning
With pep and enthusiasm it never seemed boring

The moon climbed and struggled each night
Another twelve agonizing hours of this same old life

The sun would hate when she'd set
Felt like her job was incomplete leaving upset

The moon was filled with joy each time she'd rise
Hoping and enjoying a little reprise

This was an endless cycle for many years
The cycle of setting and rising bringing both to tears

For they lost their joy each day and night
And he decided that wasn't right
To deprive his joy his shining light
Of even a thank you for helping his plight

The moon set his mind to this goal
He'd push and pursue no matter the toll

He'd rise in the day and stay out all night
Doubling if not tripling his time to make light

But it was worth it for her
The thanks she deserved
Because without her he would have never preserved
A shred of sanity himself

He rose during the day
For little to no pay
But it was worth it for his display
Of love in a blinding breathtaking array

But the sun didn't feel the same
Felt that he was taking her flame
Blocking her one time of joy in the mundane

Stuttering and stupid
He tried to repute it
But no matter how hard he couldn't get through it

It was over and gone
Stuck there waiting for the gong

Of a grandfather clock to signal daybreak
For him to recede and find his rest is a day late

For he thought even with his darkness
It worth a try
To try and find the words to harness
The love in his mind

The moon derailed
All attempts at joy
The moon had nothing more to enjoy

He waited a year
Or two or three
Till he built up the courage to want to be free

He went up again
With the determination to ascend
In hope that he'd be able to to make amends

When he got up there
So high in the sky
He was met by a much softer glare
Sitting eye to eye

With the love of his life
The only thing that mattered
In light of his strife
She was flattered

For she knew the pain he'd always feel
When he would rise in the night having to deal
With the same old strife and lack of appeal

And yet he suffered for her
To just say I'm sorry
That no matter the weather
Or however starry

That it would only be her
The light in his life

And so
They shared their love one day each year
In a blinding display
Of true love and fear
For it would be so long for them to be so near

OVERTURE

I love overtures
Of musicals or albums
It's like it wanted to make sure
You understood it's themes and values
Or it's just a good beat

But I think about that a lot
And wonder
If my life will be a little spot
Or an overture filled with wonder

My themes and lessons
Spread out for thieves to lessen
Or condensed
For only a few to mention
Which wouldn't really be my intention

Id want it to be a nice medium
To get others to see something within them
To maybe provide a small sense of meaning
To course correct a little careening

I just want it to be a lovely overture
Filled with hatred and love
To provide a little stature
To those I'm thinking of

Someone like me
Who wanted to be
An ideal picture for all to see
Even if that fully means
Destroying what made me me

Or to someone lonely
Who admires pain
To try and make them see
There is no shame
In being on your own

I just want it to be something to be proud of
Something worthwhile filled with feeling
Even if it doesn't get me a ton of crowd love
Or is super appealing

I just need it to be there
When the rain doesn't fall
I need it to be fair
When the shame takes it all

I want it to out live me
When I'm a cold old cadaver
So when nobody digs me
I can still remember that I matter

I love overtures
Because my creativity blossoms
Its a perfect post for your
work that your lost in
Or it's just a good beat
And I think about that a lot

DON'T FEEL HOT

Don't feel hot
Know I am
But I'm not

I'm on the lamb
From the fact that I rot
In my room thinking damn

What's the plot
The point the plan
Cause I've been taught

That I'm just a sham
Not hot
Just another man

Another one in the lot
Hitting me like wham
Don't got a lot

Going for me
Average plain
But I'm starting to see
I'm like the rain

Drippy at worst
And torrential at best
Most bars put you in a hearse
And I'm here to confess

To the murder committed
Cause I hate it to go to waste
And I have to admit it
I do love the chase

Of the bars and the lines
That just work so perfectly
And the hooks and rhymes
That almost certainly

Make me a little hot
I'm not
But that's the plot

Convince you differently
So you look at me
And think eh about a three

Which is better then a two
And between you
And me that's what I see

Cause I'm not hot
Might be but I'm not
So I trot

And pace around my room
Looking for lines to make you swoon
And faint to the perfect tune
A quaint little thing to hum night till noon

Because I'm not hot
And you need something to remember
It's not a lot
But your heart might surrender

It won't

A LIFE

I've got a life
I wanna live
Past the imaginary strife
See life as it is

Be in the moment
Awestruck and gleeful
Be aware and just hold it
Happy and tearful

The good and the bad
Both remnants of the past
The cold and the sad
Memories that cast

A bright future
And happier trail
A permanent suture
That makes all others pale

In comparison
To what I have now
Finally hearing let us in
Loud and proud

Opening up
To the people that matter
And closing shut
The memories that splatter

My own improvement
Building the tower
Creating the movement
Of love and power

In myself
Which is harder then it seems
Cause the thought itself
Makes me bust at the seams

A chance to rebuild
And pick up the stuffing
A chance to shield
The parts of me worth loving

Cause I have a life worth living
And I refuse to squander anymore
A chance for a new beginning
To love and grow once more